MARK

W

MA

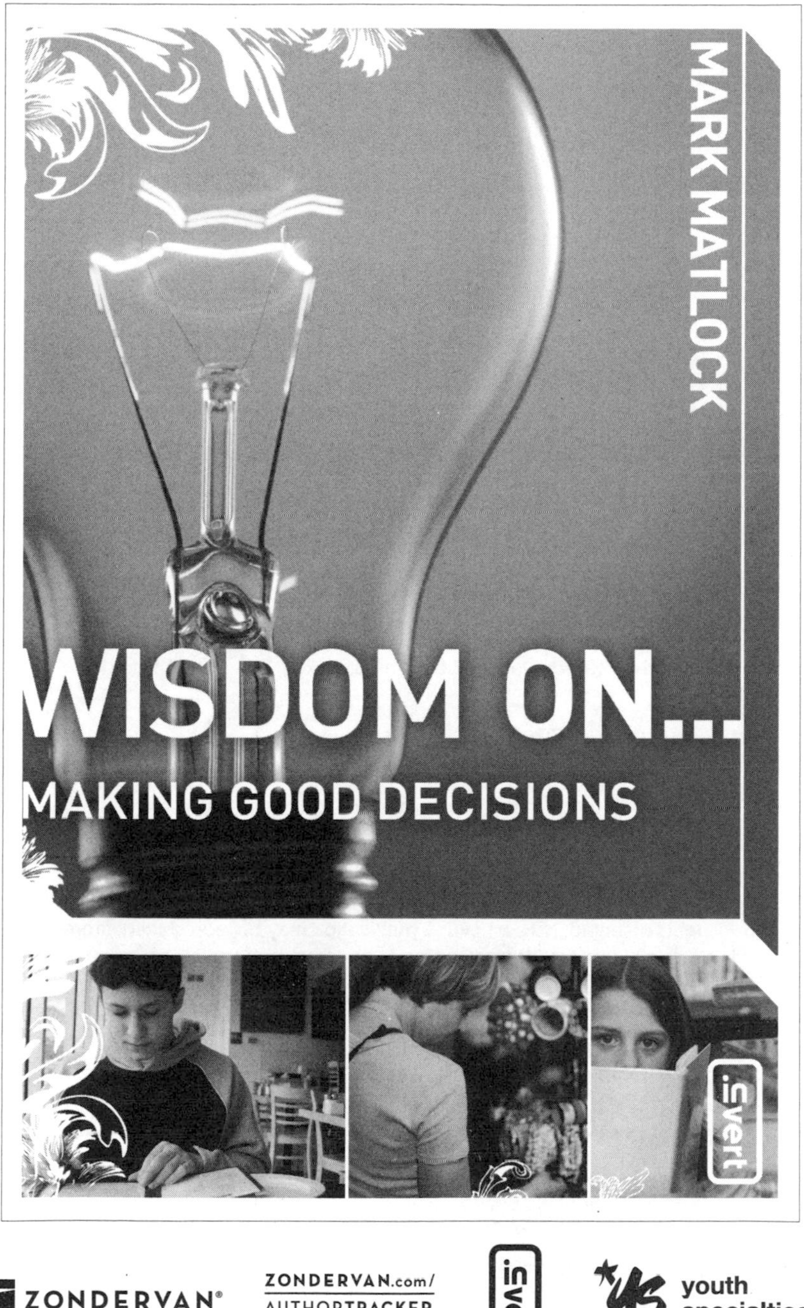

WISDOM ON...

MAKING GOOD DECISIONS

MARK MATLOCK

ZONDERVAN.com/
AUTHORTRACKER
follow your favorite authors

Wisdom On...Making Good Decisions

Youth Specialties resources, 300 S. Pierce St., El Cajon, CA 92020 are published by Zondervan, 5300 Patterson Ave. SE, Grand Rapids, MI 49530.

ISBN-10: 0-310-27926-7
ISBN-13: 978-0-310-27926-6

Cover design by SharpSeven Design
Interior design by David Conn

Printed in the United States of America

08 09 10 11 12 • 16 15 14 13 12 11 10 9 8 7 6 5 4 3 2 1

DEDICATION

This book is written for my son Dax, who will be starting middle school this year. I hope as you grow, you might read some of what your dad has written and learn from my pain.

TABLE OF CONTENTS

TABLE OF CONTENTS CONTINUED

ACKNOWLEDGMENTS

I'd like to thank my intern Jill Miller for helping put together the case studies at the end of this book. I'd like to thank Aaron Giesler and Chris Lyon for reading the manuscript and giving me feedback. I'd like to thank Randy Southern, my editor, who makes writing books easier for me and made this book more readable for everyone. I'd also like to thank Garry Friesen, whose book *Decision Making and the Will of God* brought much clarity to my study of Scripture regarding this subject.

CHAPTER 1

WALK OR RUN?

I'm not much of an athlete. Since I'm the oldest of four boys, you might assume I spent my days playing ball in the backyard with my brothers. But that wasn't me. Other than a short stint with a local soccer program, I didn't have much experience with major sports like baseball, basketball, or football when I was a kid.

When I got to high school, it seemed like most guys were playing at least one sport, so I thought I should participate in one too. But I wanted something of the non-contact variety, so that left only golf and track. And since the seasons for those two sports ran concurrently, I had to choose between them.

Golf was a game I'd never ventured to play outside of a miniature golf course. But I loved the idea of it, and I was pretty sure I'd enjoy the game. However, I was also a fairly fast runner; I thought I might excel in certain track and field events. Which to choose?

I prayed about my decision, and I asked everyone I knew for advice. But when it came time to make the choice, my major influence was my PE coach. Of all the people I knew at that time in my life, I respected him the least. While I was in his class, he called me every name in the book; he even insulted my mother a few times. This man couldn't comprehend how a 15-year-old boy had grown up without the least bit of knowledge as to how to play football. So he responded the only way he knew how: He humiliated me.

But then one day he saw me running. After I finished, he came up, put his arm around me, and said, "Son, you've got good form. You should be on the track team."

His encouragement sealed the deal. From that moment on, I determined I'd be a runner. Each day after school, I'd watch guys in khaki pants load their golf clubs onto a bus and head to the local country club to practice their putting. Meanwhile, I stayed behind to run…and run…and run to the point that I thought I'd certainly expire. And each day I asked myself, *Did I choose wisely?*

Then came the day of my first big race. I was slated to run the two-mile—eight laps around the track as fast as your body will go. It was a hot Southern California day, but I was determined to win the race and seal my spot on the varsity team.

When the starter's gun fired, I took off. After two laps, I threw up on the track. But that didn't stop me. I kept running. Did I mention how extra hot the sun was that day? Soon, I began to feel dizzy, and my side began to ache. I threw up again, spewing the rest of the French bread pepperoni pizza I'd devoured for lunch. Yet I still kept running—right up until the moment when I blacked out.

I woke up to find my feet elevated and an oxygen tube in my nose. "Wha—what happened?" I asked.

"You had a little heat stroke," my coach replied.

"Did I win?" I had to know.

My coach laughed, "Mark, you stopped about 10 feet from the finish line and let everyone pass you. What happened out there?"

I turned my head and saw the golf team getting off the bus with their lattes and cold drinks in hand. And their khaki pants looked like they'd just come from the cleaners. Meanwhile, my head hurt, and the inside of my mouth tasted like vomit.

Golf, I thought, *I should have picked golf.*

CHAPTER 2
DECISIONS, DECISIONS

Decisions come in all shapes and sizes. Some are minor and have little or no lasting impact: *What should I have for lunch? What should I do this weekend?* Others can affect your life in a major way: *Where should I go to college? Whom should I marry?* Some decisions seem minor at first, but turn out to be quite major. Others seem major, but turn out to be no big deal.

The average person makes hundreds of decisions every day, often without even realizing it. *Should I keep my cool or lose my temper? Should I speak up or keep my mouth shut? Should I help that person or ignore his need?* Those are just some of the choices we make instinctively.

Of course, not all decisions are made this way. Some require serious thought. Some involve scary leaps of faith. Some can tie your stomach into knots and keep you awake at night.

Situations like those can make you forget how amazing it is to be able to make decisions at all. Especially when you consider the alternative. God, with all of his wisdom and power, could have laid out our lives like an instruction manual: START AT POINT A. GO TO POINT B. PROCEED TO POINT C. He could have preprogrammed every moment of our lives. He could have made us robots, slaves to his commands.

But he didn't do that. When he placed Adam and Eve in the Garden of Eden, he gave them one rule: Don't eat from the forbidden tree. But then he left it up to them to decide whether or not to obey him. He gave them the *freedom* to choose.

Freedom of choice separates humans from the rest of God's creation. Animals have no such freedom. They're driven by instinct and opportunity. When an animal in the wild gets hungry, it eats whatever is available. When an animal is threatened, it attacks—or runs away. When an animal is in heat, it mates. It doesn't consider the benefits of monogamy. It doesn't make plans to meet its future in-laws.

We humans certainly have our share of instincts and drives too. But what makes us different from the animals is our capability to control our urges. Humans are able to look at situations from different perspectives. We can weigh the pros and cons before taking any action. We have the freedom to choose.

I waited 23 years—until I was married—to have sex. It was difficult, but I did it. My sex drive was strong, but it didn't overwhelm the decision-making process. I weighed the pros and cons of the situation, and I decided that my long-term purity was more important to me than any short-term pleasure.

God wants us to choose wisely. He's equipped us to choose wisely. But if we still choose unwisely, God won't interfere. Consider the two thieves who were crucified next to Jesus. (You'll find their story in Luke 23:32-43.) One thief mocked and hurled insults at Jesus. The other thief responded, in essence, "Why are you mocking him? You and I are getting what we deserve, but this man is innocent." He then turned to Jesus and said, "Remember me when you come into your kingdom."

"Today you will be with me in paradise," Jesus promised him.

One man chose to accept Jesus; the other chose to reject him. Notice that Jesus honored both choices. He didn't pressure the first thief to change his opinion. He didn't make threats. And he didn't beg. ("I really am God's Son—the only way to heaven! Please, please, please believe me!") Instead, Jesus allowed the man to make up his own mind. That's how freedom of choice works.

Of course, with freedom comes responsibility. Every choice contains an *if* and a *then: If* you choose to do this, *then* that will happen; *if* you choose to do that, *then* this will happen.

The end result is called a consequence, and it's why I'm writing this book. If you want to make wise choices, then you have to consider the consequences of your decisions. Some consequences are positive (as the faithful thief on the cross discovered), some are negative (as the other thief discovered), and some are neutral.

The good news is God has given us plenty of guidance and resources for making good decisions with positive consequences. He filled his Word with wisdom. He created us with brains capable of computing and processing the choices life throws our way. And he made it possible for us to consult and explore his will before we make any decision.

CHAPTER 3

GOD'S PLANS FOR US

Do any of these statements sound familiar to you?

> "I'm seeking God's will."
>
> "I don't want to be out of God's will."
>
> "I feel God is telling me to do this."
>
> "Just pray, and God will show you what to do."

For Christians facing a major decision, God's will is always a top consideration. The question is, *How do we know what God's will is?*

I'm not the only one asking. From students around the country, I probably receive more questions and e-mail messages about God's will than any other topic. Everyone wants to know the same thing: *How can I know God's will for my life?* Unfortunately, many people approach the question with faulty assumptions and unrealistic expectations. So rather than helping them make wise decisions, their search for God's will can actually lead them to make some very bad decisions.

I don't want you to make bad decisions or become frustrated while trying to understand what God expects from you. So let me give you some basic biblical truths about God's will.

Scripture teaches us that God has two types of plans for us to consider—his sovereign will and his moral standards. One has little to do with the choices we make; the other has a tremendous impact on our decision-making.

GOD'S SOVEREIGN WILL

The first is what we call God's "sovereign will," and it includes his plans and purposes for the universe. We see evidence of God's sovereign will in passages such as Ephesians 1:11: "In him we were also chosen, having been predestined according to the plan of him who works out everything in conformity with the purpose of his will."

However, Deuteronomy 29:29 makes it clear that, for the most part, God's sovereign will is kept secret from us: "The secret things belong to the Lord our God, but the things revealed belong to us and to our children forever, that we may follow all the words of this law."

There have been a few exceptions, of course. God has revealed certain parts of his sovereign will—often in supernatural ways through his prophets—at precise points in history (see Amos 3:7). But those revelations served specific purposes at critical times. They're far from the norm. Generally speaking, most people don't experience miraculous divine intervention in their lives.

God's ways are beyond our human comprehension. Therefore, God's sovereign will is something to submit to, rather than something to try to understand. Romans 11:33-34 suggests that a humble spirit is the best approach to God's sovereign will: "Oh, the depth of the riches of the wisdom and knowledge of God! How unsearchable his judgments, and his paths beyond tracing out! 'Who has known the mind of the Lord? Or who has been his counselor?'"

One thing we do know is that God's sovereign will rules over the smallest and largest aspects of life. When the Old Testament prophet Jonah disobeyed a direct command, God used the winds and the sea, not to mention plants and worms, to deal with him. Proverbs 16:33 takes the concept of God's sovereign will one step further by suggesting that even games of chance are under God's control: "The lot is cast into the lap, but its every decision is from the Lord."

The Bible never instructs us to try to figure out God's sovereign will before we make a decision. God's sovereign will happens regardless of the choices we make; yet it never violates our ability to choose.

Consider the crucifixion of Christ. Clearly God's will was for Christ to die on the cross for our sins. So did the people who killed him have a choice in the matter? Scripture offers evidence that God uses the freedom he's given people to accomplish his will. For example, it was in the nature of Herod and Pilate to put Christ to death. God simply used their natures to accomplish his purpose.

Acts 4:27–28 puts it this way: "Indeed Herod and Pontius Pilate met together with the Gentiles and the people of Israel in this city to conspire against your holy servant Jesus, whom you anointed. They did what your power and will had decided beforehand should happen."

This passage suggests that Herod and Pilate freely chose to do what God had determined they should do. If that seems like a contradiction, perhaps this next example will clear things up.

In the movie *Superman II,* the Man of Steel faces off against General Zod and his two accomplices. After the three villains, who are all from Superman's home planet of Krypton, escape from their prison in space, they head to Earth. Once there, they discover they have powers equal to Superman's. But, being villains, they use their powers for evil and make plans to rule the planet.

Realizing he can't fight them by himself, Superman devises a plan. First, he lures them and Lex Luthor—his longtime human nemesis who's trying to join forces with General Zod—to his Fortress of Solitude. There, in Superman's secret hideaway, he keeps a crystal that will take away the evil Kryptonians' superhuman powers. However, the problem is that this crystal will also take away Superman's powers.

Next, Superman secretly enlists Lex Luthor's help by explaining to Lex that he needs to lure General Zod and his accomplices into a specially designed chamber before he activates the crystal. But Luthor immediately betrays Superman by revealing the hero's plan to Zod.

So Zod turns the tables by forcing Superman into the chamber and activating the crystal. However, when Superman emerges, he still has his powers while General Zod and his followers have lost theirs.

Now Superman easily defeats the powerless Kryptonians, and Luthor quickly realizes what happened. The chamber was actually designed to protect Superman from the crystal's effects. Superman knew Luthor would betray him, and he constructed his plan accordingly. He didn't control Luthor, but he figured the villain's treacherous nature into his plan.

It's not a perfect analogy for the way God works in and through imperfect people, but it may shed a little more light on his sovereign will.

GOD'S SOVEREIGN WILL

1. It is secret; God has revealed only portions of it.
2. We cannot "miss it" through our decisions.
3. We're not told to seek it, but rather to acknowledge God's authority over all things.

GOD'S MORAL STANDARDS

Unlike God's sovereign will, his moral standards are completely revealed to us through his creation and his Word. One of the first pieces of evidence that points to God's moral standards is found in God's instructions to Adam in the Garden of Eden:

> The Lord God took the man and put him in the Garden of Eden to work it and take care of it. And the Lord God commanded the man, "You are free to eat from any tree in the garden; but you must not eat from the tree of the knowledge of good and evil, for when you eat of it you will surely die" (Genesis 2:15-17).

Basically, Adam was free to eat from any tree but one. God's moral standards forbade Adam from eating from the tree of the knowledge of good and evil. Adam didn't have to ask God, "Can I eat from this other tree? How about that one?" God *gave* Adam the freedom to choose, with one exception.

Unlike God's sovereign will, his moral standards can be "missed." In explaining to Adam the consequences that would follow his disobedience, God acknowledges that it's possible for people to violate his *moral standards.* Yet we have the freedom to choose *against* them.

As human history progresses, God reveals more of his moral standards. For instance, a bit later in the Old Testament, the nation of Israel receives the Ten Commandments. Every one of them is a moral standard. And through not only the teachings and example of Jesus, but also the writings of the apostle Paul and others, the New Testament reveals even more. But in the beginning, Adam and Eve had only one standard, which they violated.

GOD'S MORAL STANDARDS

1. They aren't secret; they've been revealed through creation and Scripture.
2. We can "miss" or go against God's moral standards.
3. We're instructed to seek God's moral standards in our lives.

CHAPTER 4

GOD'S MORAL STANDARDS AND YOU

What do God's moral standards mean to you as you try to make the decisions that life throws your way? Here are a couple of implications for you to consider.

YOU DON'T HAVE TO GUESS WHAT GOD WANTS YOU TO DO!

Many Christians stress out about making a decision because they wrongly believe they have to find God's one "right" answer to the problem. They spend countless hours struggling to determine God's "perfect will" for their lives—something God never told them to do.

"Perfect will"—the idea that God has a specific plan for us and that if we miss it, then we're living "Plan B"—is not a concept that's supported by Scripture. Our responsibility is to make sure we follow God's moral standards. Beyond that, we're free to choose the path for our life.

That's a difficult concept for many Christians to grasp. We want to believe that God must green-light all of our decisions—that he has a perfect will for each of us—one that we must find for ourselves. But is that really consistent with God's character and his interactions with us?

Throughout Scripture God presents himself using the analogy of a good father. Even if you don't have the best biological dad in the world, you know what a good father should be like.

I feel blessed because I do have a great father. My dad is an architect by trade, and his personality suits his chosen career. He's a very orderly, structured, and intentional person. If he weren't, then it would be hard for him to get anything built. (And if he weren't meticulous, then the buildings he designed would most likely fall down.) I see my dad as a significant creator who possesses many of God's attributes of orderliness, purpose, and imagination.

Yet as good a father as he is, my dad doesn't expect me to depend on him to make every decision for me. Can you imagine what my life might be like if he did?

> "Hi, Dad, it's me. My friends want to go to lunch. Should I go with them?"
>
> "Yes, son, you should."
>
> "Where should we go?"
>
> "You should go to Wendy's."
>
> "What should I order?"
>
> "You should order a Spicy Chicken Sandwich meal."
>
> "Should I biggie-size it?"
>
> "No, son, you must not biggie-size it."

I think you get the idea. It would be ridiculous to expect my father to have a firm opinion on all of those decisions. My father taught me how to tell right from wrong and how to make good choices. Therefore, I'm free to make decisions within those parameters without getting into trouble.

God, the best Dad we could ever hope for, has done the same thing for us. He's given us the boundaries of his moral standards and the freedom to make our own decisions within those boundaries.

YOU'LL MAKE BETTER DECISIONS

Having an incorrect understanding of God's will can lead Christians to make foolish decisions. In an effort to find the "one perfect direction" God has for each decision in their lives, people have adopted many superstitious practices that can be very dangerous. Let's take a look at a few of them.

FOLLOWING SIGNS

Have you ever played "gimme a sign" games with God? This is where you make deals with God about the decisions you need to make.

I'll give you an example from my own life. When it came time to decide on a college, my strategy was to apply to three schools: UCLA, USC, and Biola University. I convinced myself that God's sign to me would be an acceptance letter. The school that accepted my application would be the one God wanted me to attend. I felt good about my strategy, until my dad pointed out that there was a very good chance I'd be accepted by all three schools. I must admit, I hadn't considered that possibility. I was convinced God would allow me to be accepted by only the one university that I should attend. The problem was that my deal with God wasn't based on biblical principles.

On the rare occasions in Scripture when God directly intervenes in people's lives to offer guidance and direction, it's the Lord—not the person involved—who initiates contact. Mary wasn't seeking a visit from the angel who told her she'd bear the Son of God. Noah wasn't waiting for God to tell him to build an ark. Moses wasn't looking for a burning bush when God spoke to him. If God has something to reveal to us, he'll do it in his own way and in his own time. We don't need to ask for it, and we certainly don't need to wait for it. In fact, trying to interpret God's "signs" can lead to all kinds of problems.

When I was in college, a young woman told me God had given her a sign that she and I should be married. She said she'd prayed for a sign, and God had given it to her. (Apparently she didn't *ask God to share the same sign with me.) Her revelation put me in a very uncomfortable position, as I hated to see her agonize over my lack of surrender to "God's will" for our lives. Do you see the danger in following ambiguous signs?*

Gideon is one of the few people mentioned in the Bible to ask for—and receive—a sign from God. (You'll find his story in Judges 6-8.) We can learn something from Gideon's story. First, Gideon sought confirmation of a very specific message that the Lord had given him through extraordinary means. Gideon's fleece experiment was intended to remove his doubt, not to help him figure out what to do. Second, Gideon's fleece test required supernatural activity. The ground had to be dry and the fleece had to be wet, leaving no doubt that God's hand was involved. Third, Gideon tested the outcome a second time, using reverse criteria—the ground had to be wet and the fleece had to be dry.

When I've seen students play "gimme a sign" games with God, they usually go something like this: "If I'm supposed to ask her out, let her pick up the phone on the first ring," or "If I'm supposed to go out with him, let him be wearing a red shirt today." I'm sorry, but those situations aren't much of a sign—not in a biblical sense, anyway.

If you believe God will *give* you a sign, then be sure to do it right. Test both positively and negatively for a response—as Gideon did.

If you say, "Lord, if I'm supposed to ask her out, turn this water into Coca-Cola," then you'll be left staring at a glass of water. Rather than conclude that God must not want you to ask the girl out, try testing the other way too. Say, "God, if you *don't* want me to ask her out, turn the water into Coca-Cola." You'll still end up staring at water in a glass. And where does that leave you?

Another problem with sign-seeking is that we leave the "signs" open to our own interpretation. For example, a person might say, "Lord, if I'm supposed to take this class, give me a clear sign." Then if something unusual happens, he decides it must be a sign from God. However, God never insults our intelligence. He doesn't speak to people through ambiguous messages and then leave it to them to decode his meaning. When it comes to his will for our lives, why would he make things difficult and unclear? It's not in God's character to work like that.

HOOKED ON A FEELING

I was facing a major decision when I was 14 years old. I wasn't sure whether I should run for president of my school or just president of my class. Each option had some positive and some negative qualities. And I had only a few weeks to decide.

"How will I know which to choose?" I asked a Christian woman while I was at summer camp.

"You'll just know," she told me.

But I didn't know. So then I asked her, "How is it that you know?"

"God speaks to you in a still, small voice," she explained.

I listened and heard nothing. "A voice, you say? What does it sound like?"

"It isn't so much a voice as it is an inner sense that this is what you should do," she said.

That's where she lost me. A quick survey of the New Testament confirms that nowhere does God say we should seek his guidance through ambiguous feelings. Whenever God gave specific directions in Scripture (which, I'd like to repeat, was an extremely rare occurrence), he was always very clear.

The Scripture passage people typically use to support the idea of God speaking to us in a still, small voice comes from the story of Elijah in the Old Testament, specifically 1 Kings 19:11–13:

> The Lord said, "Go out and stand on the mountain in the presence of the Lord, for the Lord is about to pass by." Then a great and powerful wind tore the mountains apart and shattered the rocks before the Lord, but the Lord was not in the wind. After the wind there was an earthquake, but the Lord was not in the earthquake. After the earthquake came

> a fire, but the Lord was not in the fire. And after the fire came a gentle whisper. When Elijah heard it, he pulled his cloak over his face and went out and stood at the mouth of the cave. Then a voice said to him, "What are you doing here, Elijah?"

This idea of a "gentle whisper"—or, as the King James Version translates it, "a still small voice"—has been misinterpreted by many people to mean a "feeling" or an "impression." But as you can see, it was in fact a voice!

The belief that God directs us through ambiguous feelings such as "inner peace" is misleading and very dangerous. Some people came to my door the other day, and they tried to get me to abandon my beliefs and accept theirs. And what proof did they offer to convince me their way is true? They said I'd sense a "burning in my bosom."

God does give us peace, but not as a way to influence our decision-making process. The idea that a feeling of inner peace means God's will is being done while a lack of peace means it's not being done is ridiculous. Did Jesus have peace while he was praying in the garden of Gethsemane just before he was arrested and crucified? Luke 22:44 says he was struggling so intensely that "his sweat was like drops of blood falling to the ground." Jesus' lack of inner peace in that situation had nothing to do with God's will.

Likewise, there are times when I feel absolutely no guilt or shame in doing something I know is wrong. That peace has nothing to do with God's will. God doesn't guide us with ambiguous feelings.

MISUNDERSTANDING OPEN DOORS

In Scripture, "open doors" refers to the opportunities God gives us to do something. However, the idea that we should look for open doors or that we should go through every door that opens for us isn't a biblical concept.

Let's take a look at what the Bible does say about open doors: "But I will stay on at Ephesus until Pentecost, because a great door for effective work has opened to me, and there are many who oppose me" (1 Corinthians 16:8-9). Paul decides to continue his ministry in Ephesus because an opportunity arises that is too good to pass up.

In contrast, 2 Corinthians 2:12-13 describes a situation in which Paul doesn't take advantage of an open door—"Now when I went to Troas to preach the gospel of Christ and found that the Lord had opened a door for me, I still had no peace of mind, because I did not find my brother Titus there. So I said good-by to them and went on to Macedonia." This passage shows how the Lord opened a door for Paul to minister in Troas, but Paul was worried about Titus, so he went to Macedonia instead.

What's striking about this passage is that nothing in it suggests that Paul was outside of God's will when he chose not to stay in Troas. When God opens a door, he offers an opportunity that we may or may not choose to pursue. It's not a matter of right and wrong; it's a matter of personal preference.

I counseled a young woman who'd been given many opportunities to serve God. But this was a problem for her because she was trying to do them *all*. I asked her why she was stretching herself so thin, why she was making her life chaotic by trying to do so many things. "Because God opened the door, and I want to be in his will," she responded. In reality, she wasn't doing any of her duties well because she was exhausted from trying to do all of them. Life is filled with opportunities to serve God, so we need to choose wisely the open doors that we'll go through. Remember, the fact that a door is open doesn't mean we must enter it.

You'll find you can make better decisions when you give up on misguided attempts to find God's will. Knowing that you begin the decision-making process by looking to God's moral standards and that you have the freedom to choose what you'll do beyond that puts you on solid ground when it comes to making important decisions.

Recently, at one of our summer camps, a girl struggling with her college decision approached me after hearing me talk about God's will. She had a big smile on her face. "I just realized that I have freedom to choose which college I'd like to attend," she explained. "I've been so petrified of ruining my life by choosing the wrong school. Now I realize that either school choice is within God's moral standard. I've been waiting for some answer, some sign from God about which school to attend. Thank you for helping me to release this burden from my life."

I hope that's also how you feel after reading this section of the book. But we aren't done yet. The young woman, whose name is Rachel, came back to ask me how she should use wisdom to make the best decision about which school to attend.

"I'm glad you asked," I told her. Then I proceeded to share with her the information in the next section about how to apply God's moral standards—as well as his gift of wisdom—to the decision-making process.

CHAPTER 5

USING WISDOM TO MAKE DECISIONS

Rachel was trying to decide which college to attend. At first she considered three schools. However, her dad wasn't thrilled about one of them. So following God's moral standard to "honor your father and your mother" (Exodus 20:12), Rachel took that particular school off her list. That left her with two college options.

So what's her next step? Is there any other scriptural guidance that Rachel could apply to her decision-making? The answer is yes.

As followers of Christ, we have incredible freedom. But not all freedoms are necessarily beneficial. First Corinthians 10:23 says, "'Everything is permissible'—but not everything is beneficial. 'Everything is permissible'—but not everything is constructive."

Once you apply God's moral standards to a decision, you're left with many different options. Some options are better than others, so where do you go from there?

You ask for wisdom. As I mentioned earlier, people in the New Testament rarely prayed for specific guidance from God. However, they often prayed for wisdom.

> For this reason, since the day we heard about you, we have not stopped praying for you and asking God to fill you with the knowledge of his will through all spiritual wisdom and understanding. (Colossians 1:9)

> If any of you lacks wisdom, he should ask God, who gives generously to all without finding fault, and it will be given to him. (James 1:5)

Remember the analogy I mentioned earlier about God being a good father?

My dad didn't teach his kids just about right and wrong. He also taught us how to make good decisions and how to apply wisdom to our lives.

God has given us wisdom too. The Bible is filled with it. Let's explore how to use God's wisdom when we're making decisions.

CHAPTER 6

FOUR HELPFUL PRINCIPLES FOR MAKING WISE CHOICES

Our brains love patterns, which are developed over time. When you first learned how to read, you most likely paid attention to every letter and sounded them out as you read. Reading even a short picture book required a considerable amount of time and effort. Then, as you became more familiar with words, you no longer saw individual letters but whole words. A pattern developed. Pattrns mke it pssble to rd ths sntnce evn thgh it's mssng lettrs.

When it comes to making decisions, you use patterns as well. In fact, patterns can help us make incredibly quick and—often—good judgments. When you go out to a favorite restaurant, you're likely to order the same menu item if you've had good experiences with it in the past. And we all have our favorite clothes and our favorite beverages—all as a result of the patterns we use in our decision-making.

Inside our brains are neurons that fire every time they're stimulated. Neurons firing together form these patterns. Think of it as a field of grass. When you walk through it the first time, you mash down a path. When you walk through it again, you'll likely follow the same path you made the first time through. Over time, the more you use the path, the more permanent it becomes. In decision-making terms, the more often you make a certain kind of choice, the more likely you are to make that choice again in the future.

Our brains process both reason and emotion—and we have patterns attached to both. Emotions can be very important in making choices. However, some emotional patterns can send us off track. Perhaps that's why the book of Proverbs says, "Guard your heart above all else, for it determines the course of your life" (Proverbs 4:23, New Living Translation).

If you form good and healthy thought patterns, you'll have an easier time making good decisions. Therefore, it's important to understand the patterns that influence our decision-making and, if necessary, replace them with better patterns.

While studying the book of Proverbs (a collection of good patterns), I found some principles that can help us make good decisions. If you put them into practice, they may become patterns that you incorporate into your life. And although I explain them as "steps," they don't always occur in sequence.

Let's go!

STEP 1: DON'T ACT IN HASTE

Most poor choices occur when we make decisions too quickly. Our efficient, pattern-loving brains want to make rapid judgments—even though they're not always the best kind. So the first, and often most challenging, step in decision-making is realizing we don't have to rush to make most choices. However, many rushed decisions are the result of other people putting pressure on us to hurry up and make a choice.

Advertisers spend billions of dollars annually to hook impulse buyers. Stores want you to make instant decisions. They know that if you have time to think about a purchase, you may not buy. That's why they urge you to "Hurry!" and "Buy it now!" and "This offer is only good while supplies last!" Note: Many smart people suggest that you never buy anything that costs more than $100 until you've given yourself at least a day to think about it. That's good advice. (My wife wants it tattooed on my forehead!) Waiting is often a really smart choice.

I went to college with a really pretty, really sweet girl. One day at church she met a guy who was in the military and heading overseas. She soon fell in love with him, and they talked on the phone every day while he was away. Months later, he came back for a short stay to see her. She told me they were going to get married. She was so excited! I assumed they'd wait a year or so, but she said they were getting married right away.

I asked her, "What do your parents think about him?"

"They think it's a terrible idea for us to get married," she replied.

I looked her square in the eyes and said, "Guess what? I agree with your parents! It is a terrible idea! You hardly know the guy. Give it some time. If it's right and real, it will be right and real later on, too."

A short time later, I noticed she wasn't in school, and I got a little worried. I tried to track her down, but nobody knew where she was. I eventually called her parents' house to check on her. Her mother said, "Isn't she at school?" Her parents had no clue where she was.

As it turned out, my friend had gone to Las Vegas to marry her boyfriend. Her parents were outraged, but they didn't know what to do. And then my friend had to drop out of school during her freshman year.

But that wasn't the worst part. A few days after she eloped, my friend got a call from the military police. They told her she wasn't the only woman who was currently married to her new husband. This guy had told my friend he was divorced. However, the divorce proceedings had never been legally finalized. So the military command ordered him to annul his latest marriage or face a dishonorable discharge from the military. So what did my friend's "spouse" do? He dropped her like a bag of stale potato chips; and my friend was devastated by his betrayal and lies. (Remember, she'd already consummated her marriage.)

Proverbs 19:2 says, "It is not good to have zeal without knowledge, nor to be hasty and miss the way." In other words, it's not good to jump into something without having knowledge about it. The first question you need to ask yourself is, *How much time do I have to decide?* Then take your time. If somebody tries to rush you into making a decision, let that be a red flag to you.

STEP 2: GATHER INFORMATION

Many decision-makers never get to Step 2 because they make impulsive choices based on instinct, rather than on reason, reflection, and helpful advice. While that may seem like a decisive approach to life, it's actually a pretty lazy one. When you rely only on your own knowledge and opinions, you limit your options. However, when you seek out additional information and outside opinions, you expand your options.

Sometimes the information-gathering step is easy and straightforward because the facts are laid out right in front of you. Other times, though, the process is difficult and slow-going. It involves more than just asking a friend what she thinks.

Proverbs 18:17 says, "The first to present his case seems right, till another comes forward and questions him." One day when I was a kid, my father and I learned that lesson the hard way. The problem started when my little brother Jonathan decided to beat up my twin brothers—both of them. Despite the fact that they were seven years old and he was only three, Jonathan started whaling on them. He pulled their hair, and he knocked them down until they started crying. It was hilarious!

When my dad ran into the room, he saw my twin brothers crying, and he saw me laughing hysterically. He quickly jumped to the conclusion that I was the one who'd caused the problem! So he took off his belt and started hitting me. Suddenly, I wasn't laughing anymore.

I screamed, "I didn't do it! I didn't do it!"

Dad glared at me, and then he demanded, "Yeah? Then why were you laughing?"

When I explained to him what had actually happened, my dad felt really bad. He was putty in my hands. (I thought,

This would be a really good time to hit him up for a new computer!)

"The first to present his case seems right, till another comes forward and questions him." It's important to examine all available facts before reaching a conclusion.

Wise people are able to see issues from more than one point of view. Even if another person's point of view is flawed, it's important to be able to understand why that person might think that way.

Several years ago there was the *What Would Jesus Do?* movement. The idea was to think about life from Jesus' perspective. I like to take the process a step further and ask the same question regarding other people whom I either know personally or just know something about them. For example, I might ask, *How would my brother look at this situation?* or *What would my parents do if they were in my position?* or *What would Albert Einstein do?* or *How would Leonardo da Vinci tackle this opportunity?*

Learning to consider other people's perspectives can be extremely beneficial. For one thing, it helps us to be less self-centered. For another, it helps us learn to expand our options when we face certain situations.

Sometimes the information-gathering step requires more than just thinking about different perspectives. Sometimes it involves physical research. For example, I recently purchased an Apple computer, and I did so partly because I want to edit our family's videos. However, I soon discovered that my video camera didn't work with the Mac. The camera was too old.

So I went out to purchase a new video camera. The salesperson at the electronics store showed me a camera that featured the latest advancements in video camera technology. But when I asked if it was compatible with the Mac, he looked at the box and then stumbled over his answer. That's when I lost any confidence in his advice.

That's also when I took a moment to walk through my decision-making process. I realized I didn't need to purchase the camera at that moment, even though I was anxious to get started putting some videos together. I decided I could wait until I got more information.

I went home and got online, where I found several blogs that said the camera the salesperson had showed me did not, in fact, work with my new computer. I also learned that the ideal camera for me was actually several hundred dollars cheaper than the ones

I'd been looking at. In the end, a little physical research helped me make a good decision.

If you're facing a decision that requires some physical research, here are a few tips.

MAKE GOOD USE OF INDEX CARDS

When you have a decision to make, it helps to see nuggets of relevant information in front of you, rather than having them bounce around in your head.

Let's say you're trying to choose an elective for next semester. Your choices include sewing, cooking, woodshop, and computer programming. Your first step should be to write down the facts about your options, one fact on each index card.

Here are some examples:

- Woodshop is only available during third period.
- I hate woodshop.
- The cooking teacher is really fun.
- My friend wants to take sewing.
- I've signed up for a lot of hard classes next semester.

Once you've filled several cards, divide them into categories. For example, cards that say, I'VE ALWAYS WANTED TO SEW, MY FRIEND WANTS TO TAKE SEWING, and SEWING HAS VERY LITTLE HOMEWORK should be grouped together.

After you've grouped your cards, you may realize that you need some more information, but it's not available off the top of your head. That's okay. Do some research. In the case of our elective example, you might talk to students who've already taken the classes you're considering taking. And as you get more information, add more cards.

WEIGH THE PROS AND CONS

You may be able to reach a decision after just writing and grouping the cards. But if not, then try my second tip—weigh the pros and cons of each option. At the top of separate sheets of paper, write the title of each option you're considering. Then under that heading, make two columns—one for the benefits of that option (the "Up" column), and one for the negative aspects of that option (the "Down" column). Next, fill in the lists, using the information on your cards.

If you were facing the situation in our example, you'd use four sheets: one for woodshop, one for sewing, one for cooking, and one for computer programming. Then you'd fill in your lists accordingly.

SEWING CLASS	
UP	DOWN

Computer programming requires a lot of homework—that probably belongs in the Down column (unless you love homework and can't get enough of it). Sewing class requires little homework—this should go in the Up column. My friend is taking the sewing class—this one could be either Up (the two of you would have fun together) or Down (you might distract each other). You decide to put it in the Up column.

After you've finished your lists, take a look at the results. You'll find that being able to see all of the thoughts that were once floating around in your head is very helpful. Let's say you decide sewing class has the most potential for you, based on your lists of Ups and Downs, and you decide to take that class. If something changes—for example, if the sewing class is full—then you still have enough information to make an alternate decision.

MAKE SOME CHANGES IN THE DOWN COLUMN

If your decision still isn't clear-cut, check to see if there's a way you can "fix" anything in the Down columns. Sometimes you may be able to minimize or reduce certain negative aspects just by making an adjustment. For example, if you wanted to take computer programming, you could adjust your schedule and free up some time to work on the extra homework the class requires.

Finally, if you still have trouble deciding whether your Ups outweigh your Downs, try rating the items on your lists with a number between 1 and 10, based on how significant they are (with 1 being not important at all and 10 being extremely important). If you give each of the seven items on your Up list a rating of two and all three items on your Down list a rating of seven, then the total score of 21 in the Down column versus 14 in the Up column is a pretty strong argument against pursuing that option.

HOW WILL MY DECISION AFFECT OTHERS? We can use similar strategies to determine how a decision will impact other people. That's an important consideration, because God instructs us to care about others just as we care about ourselves (Leviticus 19:18).

Let's say your family is taking a trip to visit your grandmother who lives in another state. Unfortunately, that trip conflicts with your youth group's summer camp. Your parents say it's your choice—you can either go with them or go to camp.

Your first step in making the decision is to list on two separate index cards the names of the people who'll be impacted by each of your two options—"Go to Grandma's" and "Go to Camp."

In this case, those names might include your mom, your dad, your brother, your grandmother, your best friend, a new friend who's going to camp for the first time, and, of course, you.

Ask yourself which of those people would be happy if you went on the family trip. Your grandmother certainly would, since she hasn't seen you in almost a year. And you'd like to see her, too. However, you know you'll see her two weeks later at your cousin's wedding. You also know your mom would like to have the whole family together, even though she gave you the freedom to choose.

Now think about who'd be happy if you went to camp. Certainly your best friend and your new friend would like you to go to camp with them. Your brother might prefer it, too, since that would give him the entire backseat of the car during your family's trip. And going to camp has always been a meaningful experience for you in the past, so you'll definitely be happy if you go to camp.

The next step is to consider who might be *hurt* by your decision. Let's start with the family vacation. If you choose to go with your family, the only family member who might suffer is your brother, who'd probably like to have the whole backseat to himself. As for the other people on your list, your best friend would definitely miss you, but he probably wouldn't be devastated if you didn't go to camp. Your new friend, however, presents a different challenge. You're the only one who makes an effort to help him feel comfortable in your youth group. If you don't go to camp, your new friend may choose not to go.

On the other hand, if you do choose to go to camp, your mom's feelings might be hurt. You aren't certain how your grandmother will feel, but you're pretty sure she'll be disappointed if she doesn't get to see you. You also realize that your brother, as much as he denies it, will be bored out of his mind if you don't go along on the family trip.

After considering your options, you decide that spending a week apart from your best friend isn't as bad as losing time with your grandmother (who's getting older and whom you don't see very often). You feel bad for your new friend, but you decide to help him make some connections (maybe with your best friend) before camp so he won't stay home and miss out on the opportunity. You decide to go on the family vacation.

REMEMBER—YOU'RE NOT RESPONSIBLE FOR THE HAPPINESS OF OTHERS

As you consider how your decisions will affect others, remember that while you're responsible "to" people, you're not responsible "for" people. You can make yourself available to help them; but ultimately, they're the ones who make the decisions for their lives—for better or worse. In other words, you aren't responsible for other people's happiness.

Throughout your life you'll have friends who make terrible choices and friends who pressure you to help them achieve their own well-being. That's called *manipulation*. Don't let it happen to you. Obviously you want to show love to the people who are closest to you—but not to the point that you're being abused in the process.

Not all decisions have facts that can be gathered easily, but it's important to gather whatever information you can and consider different perspectives as you seek to make good decisions.

STEP 3: EVALUATE YOUR MOTIVES

Proverbs 12:15 says, "The way of a fool seems right to him, but a wise man listens to advice."

Motives are tricky. They're often deceptive and difficult to uncover. Ten people can do the same thing, but they might do it for ten different reasons. Yet motives are tremendously important. In the Sermon on the Mount, Jesus encouraged his followers to pray, fast, and give—but not so that anyone else would know they were doing those good things (see Matthew 6:1-18). He knew that too often we do things—even good things—for selfish reasons.

Human beings are masters at rationalization. A song from a few years ago tried to rationalize a person's desire for sex with these words: "How can love be wrong when it feels so right?" We often assume something is right just because we want to do it. But that attitude is no different from animal instinct. We just have prettier words to describe it, such as *passion* and *romance* and *desire.*

Some people think they can get away with anything as long as they attach God to it. I've talked to teenagers who tried to tell me, "I know God wanted me to have sex."

So I asked, "How do you know that?"

"I just know," came the reply.

Sometimes reason takes a backseat to raw selfishness. I've talked to young people who've stolen things, and when they were caught, they came up with this brilliant explanation: "I needed it more than he did." That's deep.

All of our decisions seem right to us initially. It's only later that we realize just how stupid or short-sighted they really were. What's more, many of us are masters at twisting words to make our actions sound reasonable. If you're uncertain about your motives for making a certain decision, ask yourself these questions:

· *How strongly do I feel about one solution over another?*

· *Am I so biased toward one decision that I'm not open to other ideas?*

· *Do I know deep inside that my desire is wrong?*

While it's difficult to uncover every bias, it's good to force yourself to think about some of the ways in which you're influenced. If you're not sure how strong your biases are, answer the following questions:

1. Do you typically favor one political party? If so, then in just one sentence, explain why.

2. Are there people in your life whose side you'd take even if they're wrong?

3. List the five worst sins a person can commit.

4. What quality do you admire most in people?

5. Why do you dress in the style you do? With what look do you identify the most?

6. Which is more important to you: finishing a task or interacting with someone?

7. Do you typically prepare in advance or do you wait until the last minute?

8. If you're supposed to meet someone, how late can the person be before you get annoyed with her?

9. What kinds of people make you cringe inside?

10. What do you think about people from other ethnic backgrounds?

Which groups do you admire and which do you not respect? Explain your attitude in one sentence.

Once you answer these questions, you'll find that you definitely have opinions on some matters—sometimes strong, emotionally driven opinions. Take a moment to reflect on how that might bias you in a given situation.

STEP 4: SEEK GUIDANCE

Once we've gathered information and achieved a better understanding of our motives, we're in a good position to seek some outside guidance regarding the decisions we make.

Proverbs 21:30 says, "There is no wisdom, no insight, no plan that can succeed against the Lord." So it makes sense that we'd put what we've learned about God's moral standards into practice first.

GUIDANCE STOP 1: PRAY FOR WISDOM

Does God want us to make wise decisions? You bet he does! In fact, he promises to give us the wisdom we need. James, the half-brother of Jesus, wrote, "If any of you lacks wisdom, he should ask God, who gives generously to all without finding fault, and it will be given to him" (James 1:5). We can be confident that God will answer our prayers when we ask for wisdom. This passage doesn't tell us exactly *how* God will deliver his wisdom to us, but it assures us that we'll receive it if we ask for it. Before we go to other sources of wisdom, we should ask God for his direction first.

GUIDANCE STOP 2: CONSIDER WHAT YOU KNOW ABOUT GOD'S MORAL STANDARD

If you're serious about applying God's moral standards to your decision-making process, the most logical place to start is with the two commands Christ gave us in Matthew 22:37-40:

1. Love the Lord your God with all your heart, soul, and mind.

2. Love your neighbor as yourself.

If those are too general for you, try the Ten Commandments in Exodus 20. Here's how Paul summarized them in Romans 13:9-10.

> The commandments, "Do not commit adultery," "Do not murder," "Do not steal," "Do not covet," and whatever other commandment there may be, are summed up in this one rule: "Love your neighbor as yourself." Love does no harm to its neighbor. Therefore love is the fulfillment of the law.

Disobedience of Christ's commands (and the Ten Commandments) can show up in many different forms. Consider the following list from Galatians 5:19-21:

> *The acts of the sinful nature are obvious: sexual immorality, impurity and debauchery; idolatry and witchcraft; hatred, discord, jealousy, fits of rage, selfish ambition, dissensions, factions and envy; drunkenness, orgies, and the like. I warn you, as I did before, that those who live like this will not inherit the kingdom of God.*

Of course, that's just the start. On the next few pages, I've listed some additional elements of God's moral standards that we should factor in to our decision-making, as well as some relevant Bible passages and key questions to consider.

SALVATION

"This is good, and pleases God our Savior, who wants all men to be saved and to come to a knowledge of the truth" (1 Timothy 2:3–4).

We know that universal salvation isn't part of God's sovereign will because not all people will put their trust in Christ. However, salvation is part of his moral standard. God wants people to acknowledge that Jesus Christ is their Lord and Savior.

Decision-Making Questions: Will my decision introduce others to Jesus? Will it create an obstacle or stumbling block that keeps people from knowing Jesus?

HONORING PARENTS

"Children, obey your parents in the Lord, for this is right" (Ephesians 6:1).

Your parents' opinions matter to God. Showing your father and mother respect and consideration in the decisions you make is important. Parents aren't perfect, of course. Sometimes giving them honor and obeying them is difficult. However, obedience is the greater good. While you're under the authority and provision of your parents, you honor God by doing what they ask.

I'm often asked, "What if my parents ask me to do something illegal or something that will harm me?" In that situation, your job is to seek help from someone who has authority over your parents. Remember, it's not God's will for you to endure abuse.

Decision-Making Question: Will my parents be pleased with my decision?

BEING FAITHFUL

"Now it is required that those who have been given a trust must prove faithful" (1 Corinthians 4:2).

We have a moral responsibility to be good stewards with the money and relationships that have been entrusted to us. That means we should be responsible with people and resources (like money or possessions) and utilize them in ways that honor God and benefit others.

Decision-Making Questions: Will my decision make the best use of what God has given me? Will it allow me to make God known and to show love to others?

CRAVINGS OF THE BODY

"You, my brothers, were called to be free. But do not use your freedom to indulge the sinful nature; rather, serve one another in love. The entire law is summed up in a single command: 'Love your neighbor as yourself'" (Galatians 5:13-14).

"Put to death, therefore, whatever belongs to your earthly nature: sexual immorality, impurity, lust, evil desires and greed, which is idolatry" (Colossians 3:5).

"For everything in the world—the cravings of sinful man, the lust of his eyes and the boasting of what he has and does—comes not from the Father but from the world" (1 John 2:16).

Animals act on their impulses. But as humans, we have a responsibility to demonstrate self-control in a way that shows love to God and to others. So even though we may have a strong sexual impulse or desire for something, we must still choose to do what is right.

Decision-Making Question: Is my decision a response to my bodily needs, or do I need to exercise more self-control?

GREED

"For of this you can be sure: No immoral, impure or greedy person—such a man is an idolater—has any inheritance in the kingdom of Christ and of God" (Ephesians 5:5).

Everything about God reveals his generosity to us. Likewise, God wants us to be generous to others. When we're greedy, we put possessions above people and, ultimately, God.

Decision-Making Question: Is my decision motivated by how much I will gain?

STATUS

"Live in harmony with one another. Do not be proud, but be willing to associate with people of low position. Do not be conceited" (Romans 12:16).

Many people will do anything to get ahead. We, on the other hand, must never make a decision that separates us from any other group of people, regardless of their status.

Decision-Making Questions: Is my decision based on a desire to show off for a group of people I want to like me? Is my decision based on a desire to avoid people I believe are beneath me?

PRIDE

"But he gives us more grace. That is why Scripture says: 'God opposes the proud but gives grace to the humble'" (James 4:6).

Many decisions we make are based on pride. We're concerned about how we appear to others. We make choices so as not to look weak or poor or hurting. God, however, wants us to base our decisions on how we can help others.

Decision-Making Questions: Am I too concerned about how this decision will make me look in other people's eyes? Am I being humble?

SEXUAL PURITY

"Do you not know that he who unites himself with a prostitute is one with her in body? For it is said, 'The two will become one flesh'" (1 Corinthians 6:16).

"It is God's will that you should be sanctified: that you should avoid sexual immorality" (1 Thessalonians 4:3).

Whether it's determining how we'll use our bodies for sexual gratification or what movies, music, and MySpace wallpaper we choose, God wants us to behave in a sexually pure manner. The words *sexual immorality* refer to *all* sexual misconduct outside of marriage, not just sexual intercourse.

Decision-Making Question: Will this decision help me maintain sexual purity?

LAZINESS

"And we urge you, brothers, warn those who are idle, encourage the timid, help the weak, be patient with everyone" (1 Thessalonians 5:14).

We sometimes make decisions based on what's easiest. While it's foolish to overwork, we must also be sure that we aren't being lazy or idle in life. God wants us to make choices that allow us to be used by him to share his message with others.

Decision-Making Question: Am I simply choosing the easy way out?

HONORING COMMITMENTS

"Above all, my brothers, do not swear—not by heaven or by earth or by anything else. Let your 'Yes' be yes, and your 'No,' no, or you will be condemned" (James 5:12).

God wants us to be people of our word. He'd rather have us say no and mean it than say yes and break our word.

Decision-Making Question: Will my decision cause me to break my word or commitment to another person?

KEEPING MARRIAGE VOWS

"For this reason a man will leave his father and mother and be united to his wife, and the two will become one flesh" (Ephesians 5:31).

"'Haven't you read,' he replied, 'that at the beginning the Creator "made them male and female," and said, "For this reason a man will leave his father and mother and be united to his wife, and the two will become one flesh"? So they are no longer two, but one. Therefore what God has joined together, let man not separate'" (Matthew 19:4-6).

Marriage is an important commitment; but because we're sinful people, some marriages don't last. However, divorce and separation are not God's desire for our lives. Therefore, the decisions we make should reflect our commitment to marriage.

Decision-Making Question: Does my decision honor my present or future marriage relationship?

Beyond God's moral standard, we have freedom. And since wisdom is a necessary companion of freedom, we must keep a large supply of wisdom handy.

GUIDANCE STOP 3: GET ACQUAINTED WITH PROVERBS

The Old Testament book of Proverbs is filled with practical wisdom for living life excellently. If you want to learn to make wise decisions, check out the collection of short statements found in Proverbs 10-29. Write down any and all statements that apply to your situation.

You don't necessarily have to go through all 19 chapters of Proverbs every time you face a decision. You'll likely find plenty of advice to help you if you read just 20 minutes at a time in the book.

Let's see how the wisdom of Proverbs applies to a real-life scenario. Here's a dilemma that one of my online friends shared with me:

> It was New Year's Eve '06, and I was at a party (which, I was under the impression, wouldn't include drinking). There was a ton of people there who were drunk and who kept trying to get me to take a shot with them. There was so much running through my mind.
>
> "Come on!" a friend shouted, "It's only one shot, and if you don't take it, they'll laugh at you."

That was the situation, so what could the book of Proverbs possibly have to say about it? Here's what I found in just 15 minutes of reading:

Like a gold ring in a pig's snout is a beautiful woman who shows no discretion. (Proverbs 11:22)

He who walks with the wise grows wise, but a companion of fools suffers harm. (Proverbs 13:20)

Wine is a mocker and beer a brawler; whoever is led astray by them is not wise. (Proverbs 20:1)

He who loves pleasure will become poor; whoever loves wine and oil will never be rich. (Proverbs 21:17)

A good name is more desirable than great riches; to be esteemed is better than silver or gold. (Proverbs 22:1)

Do not let your heart envy sinners, but always be zealous for the fear of the Lord. (Proverbs 23:17)

> Fear of man will prove to be a snare, but whoever trusts in the Lord is kept safe (Proverbs 29:25)

Obviously my friend's situation required her to make her decision at a moment's notice. She didn't have time to read her Bible for 15 minutes in order to find direction. Besides, she already knew what the right choice was. What these passages could do was give her confidence that the decisions she made were evidence of wisdom. They could also lay the groundwork for making more wise decisions in the future.

If you'd like a head start on wise decision making, spend some time reading the book of Proverbs. Familiarize yourself with its nuggets of advice so you can access them at a moment's notice. The more you read and think about them, the more you'll see the truth of them in your life.

GUIDANCE STOP 4: CONSULT ADVISERS

Proverbs 15:22 says, "Plans fail for lack of counsel, but with many advisers they succeed."

Nothing beats having multiple perspectives to inform your decision-making. That's not to say that seeking counsel from other people is easy. Many people resist asking for help for several reasons—none of which is very good.

1. THEY'RE AFRAID TO HEAR THE TRUTH

Like an *American Idol* hopeful with a terrible singing voice, they don't really want to hear the brutal facts. It's easier to live in a false world built on illusion. But think about how hard you laugh when you watch awful singers audition in front of Simon, Paula, and Randy. You ask yourself, *What were those contestants thinking? Do they really believe they're good singers?* As much as it hurts, the truth is just what you need.

2. THEY DON'T HAVE TIME

Making the effort to seek out others and share your situation with them takes time. And, let's face it, none of us likes to wait. Often we prefer to take our chances with snap judgments. If you're serious about making good decisions, however, you must take the time to seek out trusted advisers.

3. THEY THINK THEY KNOW IT ALL

Proverbs 12:15 says, "The way of a fool seems right to him, but a wise man listens to advice." Some people would rather risk doing something foolish than swallow their pride and admit they're not all-knowing.

Once you get past those initial obstacles, you're left with the obvious question: *To whom should I turn for advice?* Some people look to experts who've studied certain issues for years. I once saw a talk show where a marriage expert—with a Ph.D. and all—gave couples advice on how to improve their relationships. I Googled the counselor's name, and I was shocked to discover this marriage expert had been married three times! *Is that what makes him an expert,* I wondered, *being married more often than other people?*

I'm sure this person was very learned in the subject of marriage. But I also know that a wise person isn't necessarily impressed by college degrees. A wise person is one who looks for results, not résumé material. From whom would you rather seek advice: Someone who's been married three times, or someone who's been married to the same person for 30 years? You may be able to learn things from both, but I think the person who's had a successful marriage would be the better adviser.

Another quality you want to seek in an adviser is respect for God's moral standard. More than likely, the person who demonstrates that quality will be a Christian. I'm not saying you can't receive advice from people who aren't followers of Christ. However, their values won't be completely in line with God's values, so their advice may be skewed somewhat. What's more, just because a person is a believer, that doesn't automatically mean she is wise.

Your best bet is to develop relationships with mature believers who've walked with God and who've seen him provide direction through good times and bad. Those people will likely provide incredible wisdom and encouragement for you. They'll point out specific passages of Scripture to help you. They'll pray with you and for you.

One of the greatest problems teenagers face in the church today is their limited contact with the older people in the congregation. That's not God's intention. We need to receive wisdom from people who are older and more experienced than we are.

Along those same lines, I trust that your parents love you and want the very best for you. Chances are, they've made all kinds of mistakes themselves, and they want to help you avoid making as many of them as possible. Bite your lip and listen to them! Your youth pastor and your pastor are also great sources of God's wisdom. Ask questions—and keep asking—until you get to the bottom of the issue you're exploring.

GUIDANCE STOP 5: COMMIT YOUR DECISION TO GOD

"And whatever you do whether in word or deed, do it all in the name of the Lord Jesus, giving thanks to God the Father through him" (Colossians 3:17).

Proverbs 16:3 puts it this way: "Commit to the Lord whatever you do, and your plans will succeed."

What makes a good decision?

1. It honors God.

2. It's in agreement with God's moral standard.

3. It seeks the mutual benefit of yourself and others.

4. It's best for the short-term and the long-term.

5. It's motivated by proper values.

CHAPTER 7

PROJECTION: PUTTING IT INTO PRACTICE

The last section of this book contains some case studies for you to consider. Not only can you use them to put some of your new understanding about decision-making into practice, but you can also do something I call *projection*.

Even though we're all unique, many of the issues we face in life are very similar to the issues that other people face. First Corinthians 13 reminds us that Jesus was tempted in the same ways all of us are tempted. When it comes to making wrong decisions, we all have those temptations in common.

One way to make good decisions is to consider situations *before* we face them. Thinking about a situation in advance gives us a chance to consider the possibilities without the pressure of having to make an actual, fateful decision. Thus, we're able to project ourselves into situations we may face in the future.

In the next few pages, you'll find situations that students just like you have had to face. Read through them, and ask yourself what you'd do. I've included some questions and Scripture passages to help you along the way.

THREE ACCEPTANCE LETTERS

Brady, a senior in high school, applied to five universities during the fall semester. Near the end of February, he received rejection letters from two of the schools and acceptance letters from the other three. The acceptance letters were from West Virginia University, where all of his friends had been accepted; Ohio State University, his parents' alma mater; and the University of Texas, where he'd wanted to go since he started high school.

West Virginia offered Brady a half-tuition rate for each year he attends. (In other words, half of his college career at WVU would be paid for if he accepted and attended there.)

Ohio State offered him no money. However, his parents offered to pay for the entire amount of his tuition plus the cost of his room and board if he accepted and attended there—and only there—because they believe it's the best university in the country. They won't pay for him to attend West Virginia or Texas.

Texas offered him a general scholarship of $5,000—for his first year only—if he accepted and attended there.

1. How might the wisdom of Proverbs 29:25 ("Fear of man will prove to be a snare, but whoever trusts in the Lord is kept safe") help Brady make a decision?

2. To whom could Brady go for advice or counsel in making this decision?

3. How do the words of Proverbs 3:5–6 ("Trust in the Lord with all your heart and lean not on your own understanding; in all your ways acknowledge him, and he will make your paths straight") apply to Brady's situation?

4. How might Proverbs 16:3 ("Commit to the Lord whatever you do, and your plans will succeed") help Brady with his decision?

5. What should Brady do? Why?

A BAND BUS TRIP

Amy, a sophomore in high school, has only one close girlfriend in her entire small-town school. Amy is first chair flute in her high school marching band, and she is known throughout the band for her respectable reputation.

Lately, though, Amy's been hanging out with Jasper and Lucas, two junior boys who are also in the band. Jasper and Lucas have a reputation for partying pretty hard—cigarettes, beer, pot, and who knows what else. So far, Amy has been able to steer clear of Jasper and Lucas's efforts to engage her in their weekend behavior. However, on Friday, the football team has an away game in Industrial, a town two hours away. The entire marching band travels to the game with the team, and on the way there, Jasper and Lucas announce to everyone in the back of the bus that there's no chaperone aboard. Amy, sitting in the last seat of the bus, notices the same thing.

Jasper turns to Lucas with a grin, and then they both lean over the back of the seat to face Amy. Jasper is holding a pack of Marlboros in one hand and a lighter in the other. He says, "Hey, Amy, do you want to smoke? No one will ever know."

1. How might the words of Proverbs 15:22 ("Plans fail for lack of counsel, but with many advisers they succeed") help Amy as she struggles to make a decision?

2. In what way does the truth of Proverbs 13:20 ("He who walks with the wise grows wise, but a companion of fools suffers harm") play out in this case study?

3. How might Amy's lack of friends affect her decision-making?

4. How might the truth of Proverbs 29:25 ("Fear of man will prove to be a snare, but whoever trusts in the Lord is kept safe") play out in Amy's decision-making process?

5. What should Amy do? Why?

NO BCIS THIS FRIDAY

Violet, a freshman, is enrolled in the Business Communication Information Systems (BCIS) class. It's her last class of the school day. When she was in middle school, Violet wasn't accepted by very many of her peers. However, in BCIS class, some popular senior girls have decided they like Violet and they want her to be a part of their group. That kind of acceptance is a new experience for Violet, and she really enjoys it.

The girls in this group are upright for the most part. They don't party, they make straight A's, and they all have cars. And since they've decided they like Violet, they take her everywhere with them—lunch, shopping, and movies. Violet really feels as though she's part of the group.

But one thing makes Violet uncomfortable—most of the group skips BCIS class every Friday afternoon. Alycia, the leader of the group, started the trend, and now most of the other girls follow her lead. They've been doing it for about six weeks now; and even though Mrs. Harrell, the teacher, hasn't said a word about the girls' absences, the idea of skipping school doesn't seem right to Violet. She's glad no one in the group has asked her to join them yet.

The only girl in the group who refuses to skip class is Stasia, a junior. She stays behind every Friday and attends the class despite the group's mass absence. But lately, the other girls have been giving Stasia a hard time about it during lunch—almost to the point of making Stasia cry.

During one Friday lunch period, Violet finally gets the question she's been dreading. Alycia turns to her and asks, "So, are you going to skip with us today, Violet?" Violet hesitates. "Come on, Violet," Alycia presses. "It's just this once."

1. How might the wisdom of Proverbs 16:25 ("There is a way that seems right to a man, but in the end it leads to death") apply to this situation?

2. How many options does Violet have in making this decision? What are they?

3. Could more than one of those options be right? Why or why not?

4. How might the words of Proverbs 13:20 ("He who walks with the wise grows wise, but a companion of fools suffers harm") help Violet with her decision?

5. What should Violet do? Why?

AN EXPRESSION OF ART

Since the beginning of Matt's junior year, graffiti has been showing up on one of the outside walls of his school. Initially the graffiti was nothing more than pictures of the school mascot and some harmless words. But as the year progressed, the graffiti's gotten worse—with offensive pictures and derogatory words. Now it's almost spring break, and the school's administrators are threatening to have the culprits arrested once they figure out who's responsible for the graffiti.

During lunch one day, Matt is sitting with friends he's known since middle school. When he mentions something about the administration cracking down on the graffiti, Cliff, one of the guys in the group, asks, "Hey, Matt, who do you think's doing all that graffiti?" Before Matt can respond, another one of his friends, Tyler, leans in and whispers, "Dude, it's us." The rest of them chuckle at the look on Matt's face as he puts this new information together. Tyler kicks back in his chair and says, "Come on, it's an expression of art."

Later, during the last class of the day, Mr. Richmond says, "I've been asked to announce that if you have any information about the people who are responsible for the graffiti on school property, you must immediately notify a faculty member."

1. Whose well-being should weigh more heavily in Matt's decision-making: his friends' or the school administrators'? Why?

2. How might the wisdom of Proverbs 29:25 ("Fear of man will prove to be a snare, but whoever trusts in the Lord is kept safe") factor into Matt's decision-making process?

3. What are Matt's options in this situation? Which one should he choose? Why?

4. How do the words of Proverbs 24:26 ("An honest answer is like a kiss on the lips") apply to this situation?

JUST MAKING OUT

Tony and Lindsay, both juniors in high school, have been dating for seven months. They attend different schools, but they met through their church's youth group. Tony and Lindsay love God, and they've committed to honor him in their relationship. On their three-month anniversary date, they both professed their love for one another.

Just recently Lindsay confided to her small group leader that Tony suggested they invest in purity rings. When her small group leader asked why, Lindsay replied, "Because we both love God and one another so much that we want to remain pure."

A week later, for their seven-month anniversary date, Tony drives Lindsay to a lookout point above the city. Tony cues up one of Lindsay's favorite romantic songs and leans over to give her a "happy anniversary" kiss. That initial, innocent kiss quickly becomes a full-on make-out session. Then, in the heat of the moment, Tony asks Lindsay, "Can I take off your shirt?"

1. How does peer pressure—or in this case, boyfriend pressure—play into this situation?

2. How might the words of Proverbs 29:25 ("Fear of man will prove to be a snare, but whoever trusts in the Lord is kept safe") apply to Lindsay's sudden need for a decision?

3. How might the wisdom of Proverbs 24:26 ("An honest answer is like a kiss on the lips") help Lindsay decide how to answer Tony's question?

4. How many options does Lindsay have? What are they? Which one should she choose? Why?

5. Why is time, especially as it relates to the decision-making process, so important in this situation?

SLEEPING WITH HIS BEST FRIEND?

Caroline, a senior and captain of the drill team, is dating Erik, the captain of the football team. Caroline is also part of a tightly knit group with four other girls who've all known each other since preschool. They all attend the same youth group, and they've been through Young Life together. The group is inseparable. One night Caroline invites all the girls to her house for a sleepover. All except one of them—Shelley, the junior captain of the drill team—can come.

After a really fun evening of watching movies, painting their nails, eating ice cream, and hanging out, the girls drag their sleeping bags into Caroline's room As they're all lounging around and talking, one of the girls looks at Caroline, then looks at the rest of the group. Suddenly, the room gets very quiet. Caroline looks quizzically at her friends. "What's going on?" she asks.

After a long pause, one of them says, "Caroline, I don't know how to tell you this, but we heard that Shelley told the entire drill team that you're cheating on Erik. She said you're sleeping with Erik's best friend, David."

1. What are Caroline's options in this situation? What responsibilities does she have in deciding how to respond?

2. Should Caroline's friends have shared the information about Shelley with Caroline? Why or why not?

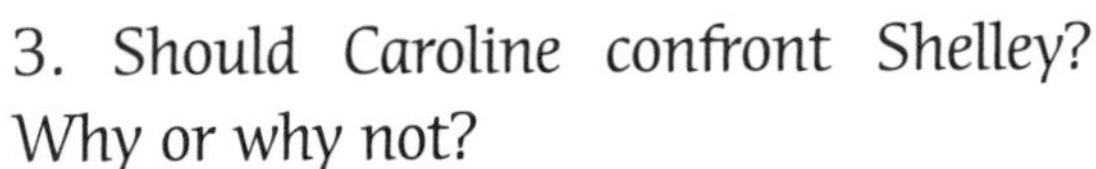

3. Should Caroline confront Shelley? Why or why not?

4. Whom could Caroline consult for advice on making a decision?

5. How might the wisdom of Proverbs 16:25 ("There is a way that seems right to a man, but in the end it leads to death") help Caroline in her decision-making process?

TWO MIDTERMS ON FRIDAY

Charli is a straight-A, honors, AP, junior in high school. She's editor of the yearbook, president of the art club, and a varsity cheerleader. Charli works part-time as a checker at a local grocery store, and she dates Michael, a senior. Good grades don't come easily for Charli. She studies hard and long for her exams. She often gets less than five hours of sleep at night because she pushes herself so hard to make the grade.

This Friday Mrs. Kenntop has scheduled a midterm in her AP English course. Unfortunately, Mr. Barnes, who's known for his horrendous honors history midterms, has also scheduled his dreaded test for Friday.

On Tuesday, three days before the tests, Charli is sitting in the library and diligently trying to keep her facts straight regarding William Faulkner and Woodrow Wilson. Michael walks in, sits down, and places several pieces of paper facedown on the table in front of Charli. "Hey, babe, you know what this is?" he asks. Charli shrugs. "It's the answer key to Barnes' midterm exam," he says.

1. How might the wisdom of Proverbs 16:25 ("There is a way that seems right to a man, but in the end it leads to death") help Charli make a decision?

2. How might the words of Proverbs 16:3 ("Commit to the Lord whatever you do, and your plans will succeed") play into Charli's thought process?

3. What are the differences between Michael's thoughts, Mr. Barnes' thoughts, God's thoughts, and Charli's thoughts regarding this situation?

4. How might considering each viewpoint help Charli make a decision?

5. What are Charli's options now? Which should she choose? Why?

FIVE-FINGER DISCOUNT

Roni is a sophomore. She just moved to a *new* school in a *new* state because her dad got a *new* job at a *new* church. Roni misses her old school and her old youth group. For three weeks, she's tried making new friends at school, but it's not going very well.

The youth group at her dad's church, however, is a different story. At her very first meeting, Roni is put at ease right away. The other girls are extremely friendly, and they invite her to sit with them during small-group time and then invite her out for lunch afterward. Roni accepts. After lunch, the girls ask Roni to join them for a trip to the mall. Roni eagerly accepts again, as she's grateful for the camaraderie.

At the mall, Anna, one of the older girls, leads the group to the Hollister store. Inside, the girls start grabbing clothes off the racks and discussing how adorable and cute everything looks. Each of them heads for a dressing room, leaving Roni alone in the middle of the store. After a few minutes, they all come out empty-handed.

Anna walks up to Roni and whispers, "What did you get?" Roni looks at her quizzically. "You know," Anna says as she lifts up her shirt just enough to show Roni the three stolen camisoles she's wearing underneath, "what did you get?"

1. What are Roni's options for dealing with the situation?

2. Is there anything Roni could have done to prevent being put in this situation? If so, what?

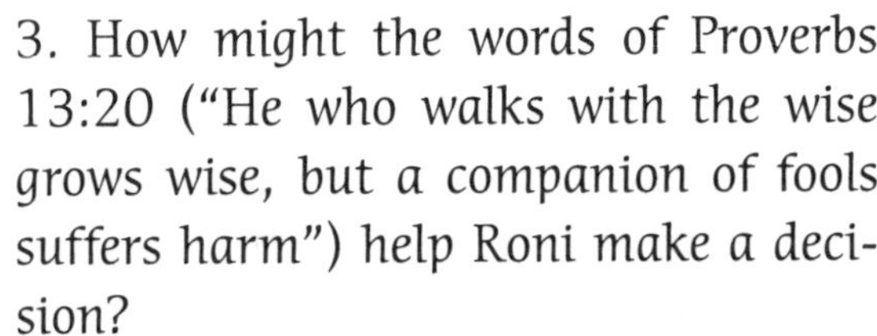

3. How might the words of Proverbs 13:20 ("He who walks with the wise grows wise, but a companion of fools suffers harm") help Roni make a decision?

4. How might the wisdom of Proverbs 29:25 ("Fear of man will prove to be a snare, but whoever trusts in the Lord is kept safe") influence Roni?

5. Based on Proverbs 23:17 ("Do not let your heart envy sinners, but always be zealous for the fear of the Lord"), what should Roni do?

LOST TRACK OF TIME

Vince, a junior in high school, just received his driver's license. His parents each have a car, but they told Vince they can't afford to buy him one of his own. However, they did offer to let him drive one of their vehicles whenever the need arises.

Vince is in the Future Scientists Club (FSC). After school on Tuesday, his eighth-grade sister, Taylor, has volleyball practice; but Vince has a trash-pickup outing for FSC. Both events last until 5:30 P.M. So Vince's parents let him drive Taylor and himself to school. They even tell him he can use the car during lunch period. Their only stipulation is that he must pick up Taylor after her volleyball practice and be home by 6:00 P.M.

Vince drives the car into the driveway—with Taylor in the passenger seat—at 7:00 P.M. His parents sit him down and ask what happened. He explains that his friends wanted to hang out a little longer after trash pickup, and he lost track of time. His parents ground him from using the car for two weeks.

1. On a scale of 1 to 10 (with 1 being "not at all important, and 10 being "extremely important"), how important is Vince's decision regarding how he'll respond to his parents' punishment? Why did you choose that number?

2. How might the words of Proverbs 15:18 ("A hot-tempered man stirs up dissension, but a patient man calms a quarrel") help Vince decide how to respond to his parents' punishment?

3. How might the words of Proverbs 17:27 ("A man of knowledge uses words with restraint, and a man of understanding is even-tempered") help him?

4. What are Vince's options? Which one should he choose? Why?

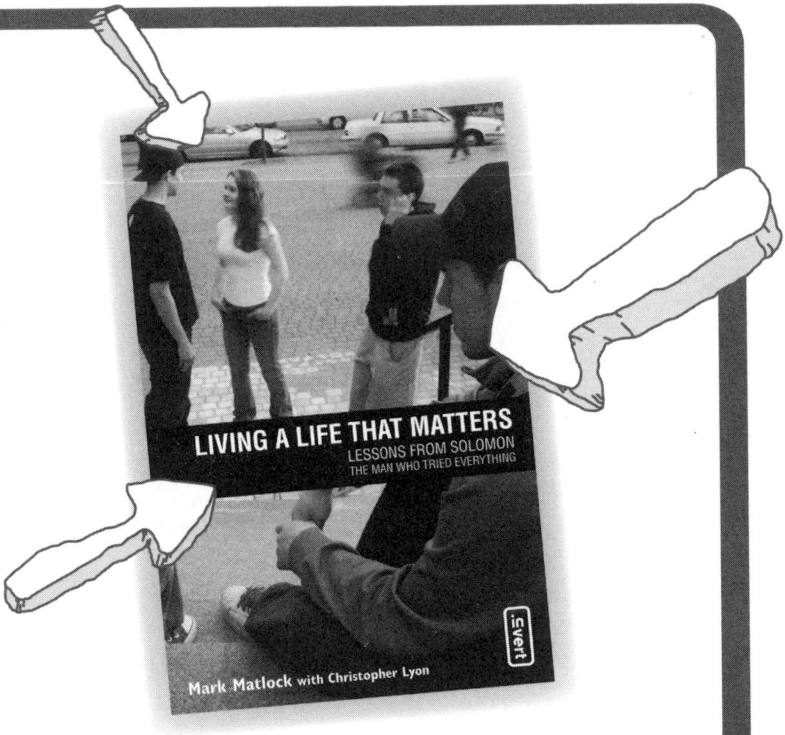